UNEMPLOYED?

Your Complete Workbook to "Life On Your Terms"

---

www.hippycapitalist.com

CHEROKEE STREET PUBLISHING

Copyright © 2020
Kris Kluver
All rights reserved.

YOUR COMPLETE WORKBOOK

UNEMPLOYED?
Underemployed, or miserably employed...

"LIFE ON YOUR TERMS"

Kris Kluver

CHEROKEE STREET PUBLISHING

Copyright © 2020
Kris Kluver
All rights reserved.

UNEMPLOYED?
Your Complete Workbook
to "Life On Your Terms"

ISBN: 978-1-64921-165-1 Ebook
ISBN: 978-1-64921-166-8 Paperback

To all the hardworking people displaced
by the COVID-19 virus of 2020.

With great disruption comes great opportunity.

CONTENTS

FOREWORD 15
INTRODUCTION 19
    THE HIPPY CAPITALIST'S CREED 22

PART I: THE BALANCE WHEEL 25
    THE BALANCE WHEEL INTRODUCTION 26
    WHAT DOES SUCCESS LOOK LIKE? 27
    LIFE BALANCE WHEEL 30
        EXERCISE: THE BALANCE WHEEL ASSESSMENT 31
        BWA: PROFESSIONAL QUESTIONNAIRE 32
        BWA: RESOURCES QUESTIONNAIRE 33
        BWA: RELATIONSHIP QUESTIONNAIRE 34
        BWA: HEALTH QUESTIONNAIRE 35
        EXERCISE: THE LIFE BALANCE WHEEL 36
        LIFE BALANCE WHEEL 37
    CONCLUSION 38
    CONCLUSION NOTES 39

PART II: VISUALIZE 41
    VISUALIZE INTRODUCTION 42
        EXERCISE: VISUALIZATION 45
        PROFESSIONAL 46
        RESOURCES 47
        RELATIONSHIPS 48
        HEALTH 49
    CONCLUSION 50

CONTENTS

PART III: LIFE-CHANGING GOAL (LCG) 53
LIFE-CHANGING GOAL (LCG) INTRODUCTION 54
EXERCISE: IMAGINE YOUR LCG 56
EXERCISE: NARROW TO ONE 59
EXERCISE: IDENTIFY YOUR LCGL 63
NEXT STEPS 64
EXERCISE: WHAT NEEDS TO BE DONE? 65
EXERCISE: NARROW IT DOWN 66
YOUR IDEAL JOB 67
WHAT IS YOUR DREAM JOB? 69
EXERCISE: VISUALIZE YOUR DREAM JOB 70

PART IV: MAKE IT HAPPEN 73
WHO CAN HELP? INTRODUCTION 74
SAME AREA OF EXPERTISE 75
SIMILAR BELIEFS 76
WHAT TO ASK? 77
QUESTIONS TO ASK 78
QUESTIONS TO ASK 79
INTERVIEWING 80
MY INTERVIEW QUESTIONS 83
MY INTERVIEW QUESTIONS 84
ACTION ITEMS 85
WHAT NEEDS TO BE DONE 86
WHAT NEEDS TO BE DONE 88
5 STEPS AT A TIME 92
5 STEPS AT A TIME 93

CONTENTS

    5 STEPS AT A TIME 94
    5 STEPS AT A TIME 95
  ACCOUNTABILITY 96
    EXERCISE: ACCOUNTABILITY PARTNERS 98

ADDITIONAL RESOURCES 101
  FACEBOOK 102
  YOUTUBE 103
  LINKEDIN 104
  STARTING A BUISNESS 105
  THE ASPIRING SOLOPRENEUR 106
  COUPLES ONLINE WORKSHOPS AND RETREATS 108
  SENIOR EXECS AND BUSINESS OWNERS 109

CONCLUSION 111

ACKNOWLEDGEMENTS 113

REFERENCES 115

ABOUT THE AUTHOR 117

FOREWORD

In 1969, my dad made $90,000. He was at the top of his career. We lived in a big, beautiful mansion in the Sand Point Country Club in Seattle. Everything was going great. On May 1st, 1970, my dad woke up with flu-like symptoms; by November 18th, he was dead. He was only 41 years old.

I've always been well aware of how short and fragile life can be, which has impacted how I viewed living my life. Because my dad was severely underinsured, his passing initiated a downward spiral for my mother and me. I ended up living in 28 homes and attending 11 different schools. My mother shipped me off to live with relatives twice, once in the fourth grade and once in the ninth grade. You can see that I wasn't necessarily set up for the greatest start in life.

However, late in my high school years, I figured out that life didn't have to be so bad. In fact, it could be truly amazing. I had a significant change during this time: I stopped going in one direction and began going in the right one. Although I had mentors off and on until then, I didn't have any in my life at that point. Eventually, I found some great mentors who taught me how to live my best life. Mentors teach us what they've already learned, so we can learn them faster. They teach us about the mistakes they made, so we don't repeat them.

Every person on the planet wants to live their best possible life. The older we get, the shorter it seems, further propelling us to live our best life.

The key to living your best life is being clear about how you want that life to look, so that you can live life on your terms. Each person has different goals and a different vision for their life than everyone else, and that's okay. Your life does not have to look like someone else's. There's no right or wrong way. There's only the way in which you want to spend your one and only life.

It's true, isn't it? Life is short and precious.

My friend, Kris Kluver, has written this extraordinary book about how you can live your best life. It's deep within all of us to make a difference and a lasting impact. Follow Kris's advice and you will be well on your way to fulfillment. I encourage you to read through this content slowly and take in the wisdom that is shared. Internalize it and apply it. By doing this, you'll cut down your learning curve, helping you to avoid potential mistakes along the way. Think of this book as a road map for charting the course to a better life.

The life that you choose.

The life that you want to live.

The life that will make you happy.

This is what it's all about. Start living your best life today with this invaluable resource!

Chris Widener

INTRODUCTION

For those of you who have recently lost your job, I say, "Congratulations."

No, I am not trying to be crass. I really mean it. According to *Gallup*[1], as much as 85% of the workforce does not like their job. *Forbes*[2] continues by stating that **"work is more often a source of frustration than fulfillment for nearly 90% of the world's workers."** I offer a celebratory message because I believe, deep in my heart, that losing your job creates an opportunity. With this newfound freedom, you can now invest the time to take a breath, define what great looks like, and decide where you want to go. If you look at it right, this really is an amazing opportunity.

Now, I can hear some of you saying, "But, dude. You don't get it. I have a family to take care of and bills to pay. And I don't like change." I promise I get it. As humans, we often struggle with change and we tend to look at the negative. I have seen people stuck in jobs they have hated for months, years, even decades – which illustrates how we can be so fearful of change that we will endure untold discomfort for long periods of time. I have also seen this fear of change on the employer's side. This happens, for example, when an employer is aware they have an employee who may not be great at what they do or perhaps they do not fit the culture, yet they continue empowering that person to fail by allowing them to stay. It all boils down to the employer's fear of change and them lacking the willingness to help the person move on.

Likewise, if you are reading this, you are probably unemployed. You are in this situation, and that will not change with a magic wand. So, how can you control the narrative in your head to approach your circumstances with positivity and excitement?

Let me be clear. This does not mean these transitions will be free from discomfort. There may be some uncomfortable times, but remember that it is okay. We tend to freak out and worry about the unknown instead of realizing the discomfort we left was likely much scarier. In moments like these, we should try to embrace a mindset of gratitude (which is not always an easy task).

Within the human brain is the limbic cortex, commonly known as **"lizard brain"**. This section of our brain is responsible for basic functions, such as our fight-or-flight responses. Many researchers believe it is the oldest part of the brain, as it helped our ancient ancestors to avoid getting eaten by saber-toothed tigers. Our limbic cortex reacts in remarkably similar ways when we perceive threats in today's world. As a result, if we lose a job, we typically behave in a frightened, reactionary way. It is okay; it is our biology. However, we can learn to take control of that narrative and spin it in a positive manner. If we fail to learn this, we are destined to end up in another job we do not love.

When asked what I do, I respond by saying, **"I help people to think differently."** That being said, my primary objectives with this book are threefold:

1. To empower you to think about what a great, balanced life looks like – for you.
2. To help you determine where you want to go next in life.
3. To transition your thinking to a proactive approach in getting your dream job.

Together, we will achieve this! We will use proven, time-tested tools I created through my leadership coaching practice and in collaboration with my wife, Reka, a couples and family therapist and life coach. Combined, we have over 60 years of professional experience, including the couples workshops and retreats we facilitate together.

To learn more, please visit us at www.hippycapitalist.com.

This process is specifically designed to help you begin to proactively approach your life and to visualize your next job. This thinking, in and of itself, may be a paradigm shift in your thinking.

In my experience, it seems that people frequently do not know what they truly want. They might even look to others to decide for them. This thinking is easily influenced by commercials and advertisements, our peer groups, our families, as well as a dozen different influencers. In virtually every case, someone has an ulterior motive. They may want to sell you something or they may have unknowingly manipulated you as a result of their own fear of change. Even those with the best intentions may be imprinting their own scared mindset or negative experiences onto you.

Think about this: Do you know someone who went into a certain field because their parents repeatedly pointed out that it paid well or that it was safe? These are great reasons with great intentions, no doubt; however, what if that individual never took the time to think about their enjoyment in performing that job? Or maybe they love the work, but not the workplace. Very few of us are willing to say we would rather take less money and work at a place that loves us. In the long run, you will be much more successful if you do just that.

Finding a good job with a wonderful company in a solid industry is all possible. Treat this like a treasure hunt. Use this book as your treasure map to help you begin living a happy life – on your terms.

THE HIPPY CAPITALIST'S CREED

A Hippy Capitalist is someone who is thriving. Someone who lives life on their terms. Someone who does not care how others define success.

A Hippy Capitalist has purposefully taken the time to define what a successful life looks like to them. A Hippy Capitalist knows the secret to success is a purpose-driven life.

A Hippy Capitalist intentionally builds a plan, step by step, to achieve their life potential and dreams.

When success is achieved, a Hippy Capitalist is proud of their accomplishments and embraces the benefits they provide. A Hippy Capitalist shares and thrives in their success and these benefits.

A Hippy Capitalist understands that life is not fair. As a self-aware Hippy Capitalist, they realize they, themselves, are the proof of this. A Hippy Capitalist embraces that they are one of the lucky ones.

A Hippy Capitalist acknowledges that life will have setbacks, and that through these challenges, life offers opportunities to learn new lessons and grow. A Hippy Capitalist loves learning.

A Hippy Capitalist is accountable, owning that the person in the mirror is 100% responsible for who the Hippy Capitalist is to today and who they will become tomorrow.

INTRODUCTION

A Hippy Capitalist learns from the past, but does not let the past control their future. A Hippy Capitalist lives in the present and loves the possibilities of the future.

A Hippy Capitalist is curious and strives to understand the perspectives of those who think differently. A Hippy Capitalist believes that different thinking, by smart people, is an opportunity to learn something new.

A Hippy Capitalist fervently protects the rights of others to think differently, even if the Hippy Capitalist does not agree with what is presented.

A Hippy Capitalist knows the power of a smile and a kind word. A Hippy Capitalist knows that for every smile given and for every person helped, the positivity that is returned grows exponentially.

A Hippy Capitalist celebrates success, lives fearlessly, dreams audaciously, and gives abundantly.

Congratulations to you for joining the movement.

Welcome to the revolution.

This book and others in this series are part of **www.hippycapitalist.com**.

PART I:
THE BALANCE WHEEL

THE BALANCE WHEEL INTRODUCTION

As a society, we tend to measure success through dollars, titles, or the size of one's house and car. The more and bigger stuff a person has is equivalent to their success, right? If someone were to describe an individual who has all of the above (and more), it may sound like, "She is so successful. She is a brain surgeon who makes $500 an hour. She lives in a huge mansion, has a second home in the mountains, drives a Mercedes, and always has the newest designer fashions." Yep, she sounds successful – and by certain standards, she is. I consider this to be left-brained thinking of success. However, what if that same brain surgeon describes her life like this?: "I hate the bureaucracy at the hospital, and I do not like going in every day. I have zero free time for myself or my family. My oldest son is doing poorly in school. I feel totally out of shape and completely burned out. And I think my husband might be cheating on me because I work all the time." Wow, different perspective, huh? It does not appear that she is living the life others thought she was living. In fact, she kind of sounds like a train wreck.

I have seen variations of this scenario repeatedly come to life. The person being referenced may be the same person, meaning they have a perspective from the outside looking in and the other deals with how they view success for themselves. By most traditional standards, they are exceptionally successful; however, the reality could not be further from the truth.

The reality is that a truly successful life most often requires people to find the balance between the right and left brain.

PART 1: THE BALANCE WHEEL

WHAT DOES SUCCESS LOOK LIKE?

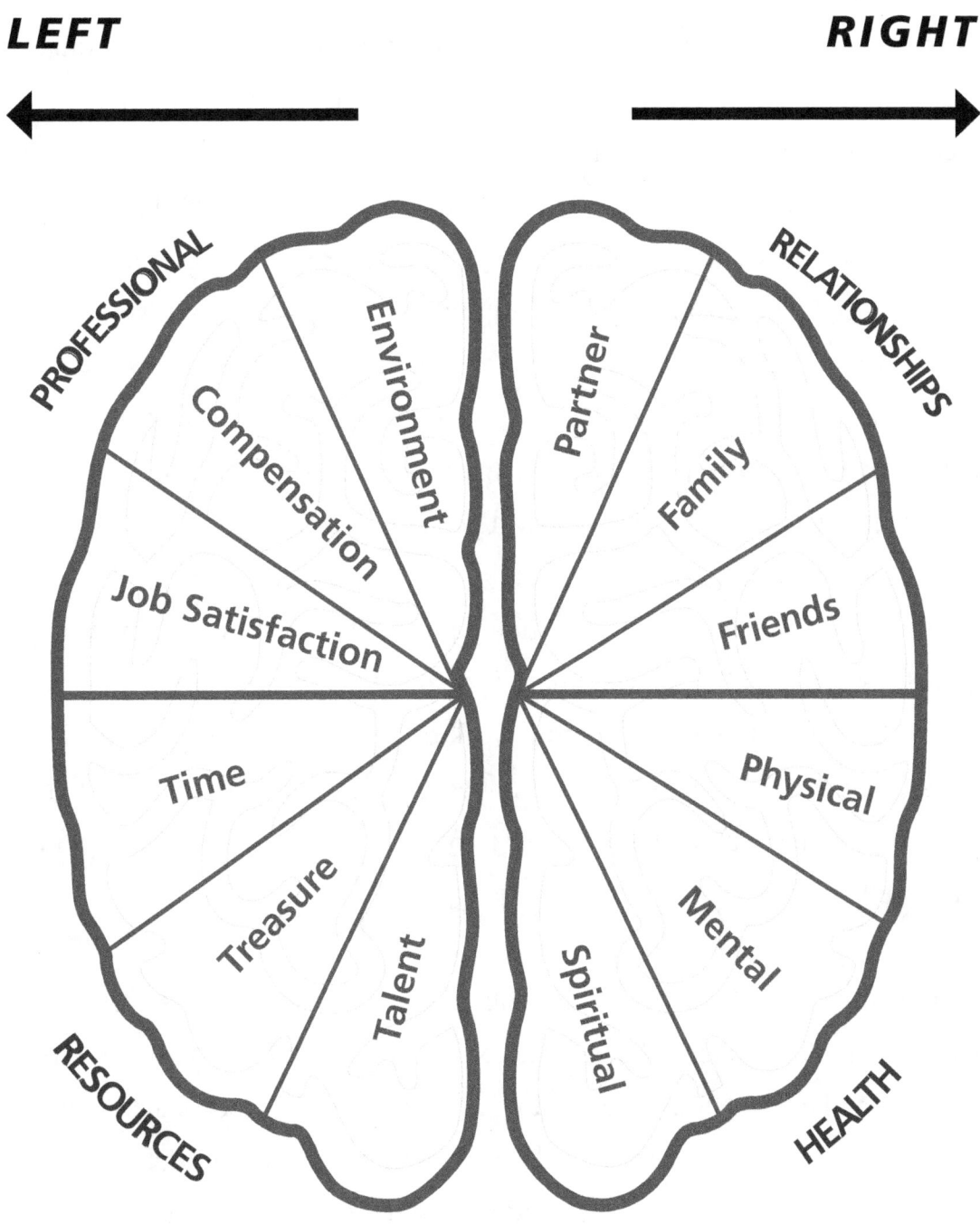

How are you defining success?

The image on the previous page shows the two hemispheres of the human brain. Notice the different components within each hemisphere. The left side is how most people over 45 years old measure success, while the right side is how many younger folks often regard success. I believe, in many cases, the younger generations (millennials) are asking the right questions. They are looking for a simpler and slower life, quality physical and mental health, as well as a trusted partner with whom they can grow. I should point out that I do not think any of this is wrong, but if you are an old guy like me, you have probably told your new, young employee, "Look, you're going to need to put your nose to the grindstone and work your way up. Eventually, say in 20 years, after working 70 hours a week, you can make partner, and you can have a house and second home like me." This is when the newbie looks at your excessive midsection then asks how many times you have been married and why your kids will not talk to you anymore.

I have also seen this scenario play out many times. Do you think that new kid is going to stick around after hearing that? Probably not. The millennial may want to do quality work they know is impactful, work only 30 hours a week, take six weeks off a year, strictly drink craft beer, have a loving relationship with their significant other, and be on the fast track to partner in five years. I consider this to be more right-brained thinking.

So, what is the answer? Obtain all the dollars and accolades and risk losing balance, or should it be moonbeams, rainbows, and hoping for the best? The reality is this: I believe neither way will work on their own. To be successful, there needs to be a balance of both sides of the brain. In order to define success on your terms, you must first understand your starting point, so you can define where to go.

The Balance Wheel is a tool I designed specifically to help people learn to think differently about success by holistically assessing their strengths and opportunities. I strongly believe that it is important to find a positive balance between right-brained thinking and left-brained thinking. As in the previous example, you may have all the money in the world, but if your home life is a wreck, it is highly likely that you are not genuinely happy. On the flipside, if you have a great home life and physical health, yet you live in your parents' basement and bounce from job to job every few months, you may have some opportunities for growth on the left brain side of the chart.

You need to have a little of both brain sides to be truly balanced – how much of each is 100% up to you.

UNEMPLOYED?

LIFE BALANCE WHEEL

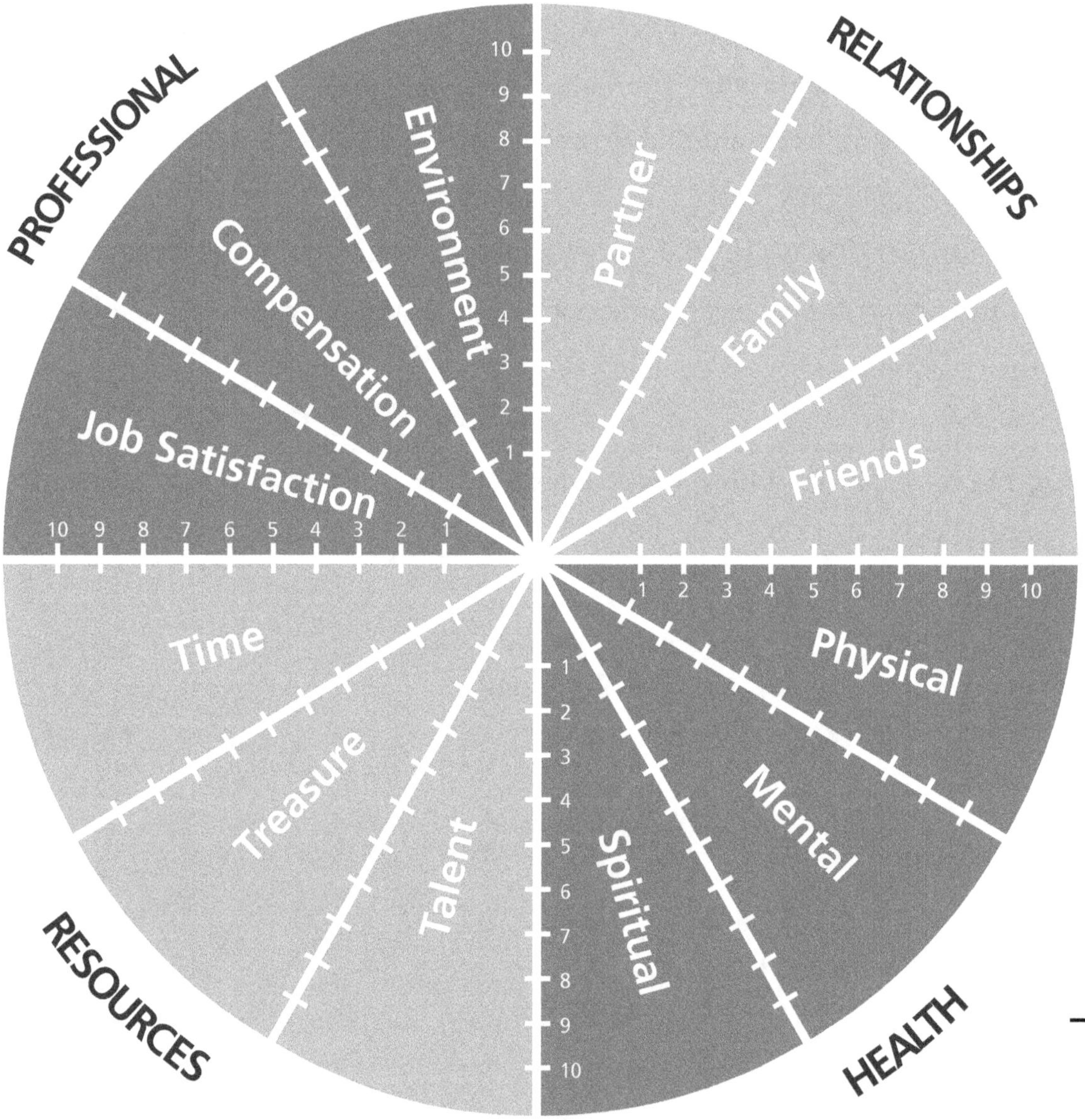

PROFESSIONAL — Environment, Compensation, Job Satisfaction

RELATIONSHIPS — Partner, Family, Friends

HEALTH — Physical, Mental, Spiritual

RESOURCES — Time, Treasure, Talent

Instructions: *Use the assessment on the following two pages to calculate your average for each subsection. For each subsection in the wheel below, draw a line to match each score.*

Example:

$$\underline{9 + 7 + 3 + 6 + 5} = \underline{30} \div \underline{5} = \underline{6}$$

Each Question's Score | Total Physical Score | # of Questions | Subsection Average

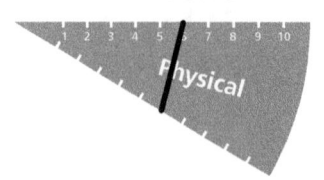

30

PART 1: THE BALANCE WHEEL

EXERCISE: THE BALANCE WHEEL ASSESSMENT

Answer the following 60 questions as honestly as possible, not how you think your spouse, parents, or the handsome hunk on the beer commercial would respond. Once you have answered all the questions, you will begin to see the shape of your wheel. Is it smooth and round? Or is it broken and missing a few spokes? Keep in mind that either is okay, as long as you answered sincerely. The shape of your wheel simply identifies areas of strength and areas for growth.

Please take the time to honestly go through each question and score them on the following pages. A score of '1' reflects that you feel there are a lot of opportunities to improve in this area. A score of '5' indicates you are pleased with how you are doing in this area. We will then review and discuss your Balance Wheel responses.

UNEMPLOYED?

BWA: PROFESSIONAL QUESTIONNAIRE

Environment.   Score:

I feel happy and comfortable in my workplace.

I like and respect the people with whom I work, and I believe they like and respect me.

I feel like my workplace supports both my personal and professional growth.

I understand the direction of the organization and how I'm contributing to achieving the overall goal.

My workplace's values align with my personal values; therefore, meeting my needs.

Environment Total: _____

Compensation.   Score:

I believe that I'm paid what I deserve for my efforts.

I have the amount of time off and flexibility I desire.

My skills are being utilized to their highest and best use.

I have a clearly defined path for growth and advancement.

I receive the level of training I want; if not, I have the support of the organization to obtain more training.

Compensation Total: _____

Job Satisfaction.   Score:

I enjoy the work I do and I like going to work.

I enjoy my co-workers.

There are specific and clear expectations of me and my responsibilities.

I have clear metrics that enable me to determine if I'm successful.

I understand how my contributions impact the overall success of the organization.

Job Satisfaction Total: _____

PART I: THE BALANCE WHEEL

BWA: RESOURCES QUESTIONNAIRE

Time.   Score:

I feel I have enough time to complete all my work and daily tasks.

I take as much vacation time as I want.

I have enough time to attend events that support others.

I invest the time daily for my own clarity and physical exercise.

I take time to invest in my hobbies and personal growth.

Time Total: _____

Treasure.   Score:

I have all the right "stuff" I need to live my best life.

I could go without an income for at least six months.

My financial stability enables me to live the life I desire.

My "stuff" (house, car, etc.) supports the life I want to live.

My financial and work lives aren't focused on supporting my "stuff".

Treasure Total: _____

Talent.   Score:

I feel I've found my true natural talents in life.

I currently embrace and utilize these talents to their full potential.

I take the time I need to develop and improve these talents.

Others are aware of the talents I possess.

I have a clear plan to maximize and benefit from these talents.

Talent Total: _____

BWA: RELATIONSHIP QUESTIONNAIRE

Partner. Score:

I'm satisfied with this relationship.

We've set clear goals and plans for our future together.

We're open and honest in our communications.

I'm supportive of my partner's needs and goals.

My partner is supportive of my needs and goals.

Partner Total: _____

Family. Score:

I'm satisfied with these relationships.

We're open and honest in our communications.

I know the goals of my family members, and I support and help them in achieving them.

I ask questions and actively listen when in conversation.

I feel I'm heard when communicating with my family.

Family Total: _____

Friends. Score:

I'm satisfied with my current level of friendships.

I'm open and honest in my communications with my friends.

I personally meet with friends at a frequency I like.

My partner and I meet with friends at a frequency we like.

I'm happy with the degree and engagement level of my friendships.

Friends Total: _____

PART I: THE BALANCE WHEEL

BWA: HEALTH QUESTIONNAIRE

Physical.   **Score:**

I'm happy with my level of physical activity and fitness.

While alone, standing naked in front of a mirror, I'm pleased with my appearance.

I invest the time daily to make my physical health a priority.

I have a good understanding of and healthy relationship with what I eat and drink.

I'm confident the vices I choose to embrace have minimal negative impact on my health.

Physical Total: _____

Mental.   **Score:**

I'm happy with my current level of mental health.

I'm pleased with who I am and am confident with where I'm going.

I like the people I surround myself with.

I rarely have feelings of dread or worry.

I invest time daily to provide myself with clarity and peace of mind.

Mental Total: _____

Spiritual.   **Score:**

I'm happy with my definition and understanding of "spirituality".

My spiritual beliefs are in alignment with how I live my life.

I've surrounded myself with others who share my spiritual beliefs.

I make important life decisions based on these beliefs.

My spiritual beliefs help me find purpose and direction in my life.

Spiritual Total: _____

EXERCISE: THE LIFE BALANCE WHEEL

Congratulations on taking a giant, proactive step forward in defining what a great life looks like for you – on your terms.

The intention of The Balance Wheel exercise is to provide you with an honest self-assessment of where you currently are in life. More importantly, this tool has been designed to prompt you to think differently about what success looks like for you. Looking at your life holistically can guide you in recognizing opportunities for growth. And I strongly believe that one of the most critical first steps in achieving your ideal life is defining where you want to go in life.

Once you start identifying your strengths and areas of opportunities, you will begin looking at job opportunities differently. This new perspective of "work" can empower you to define what is really important. Then, you can compare the values and focal areas of the potential job to your own, making sure everything is in alignment. In other words, you want to ensure it is the right fit.

I can hear some of you saying, "Dude, you don't get it. I have to get paid." I want you to know that I do get it. I realize this may be a different way of thinking, and I can promise you will be much happier if you focus on the right fit first and compensation second. If you love what you do and your life is balanced, you will excel. The financial compensation will come.

In the pie chart below, please mark your scores for each section through the corresponding wedge on The Life Balance Wheel.

PART I: THE BALANCE WHEEL

LIFE BALANCE WHEEL

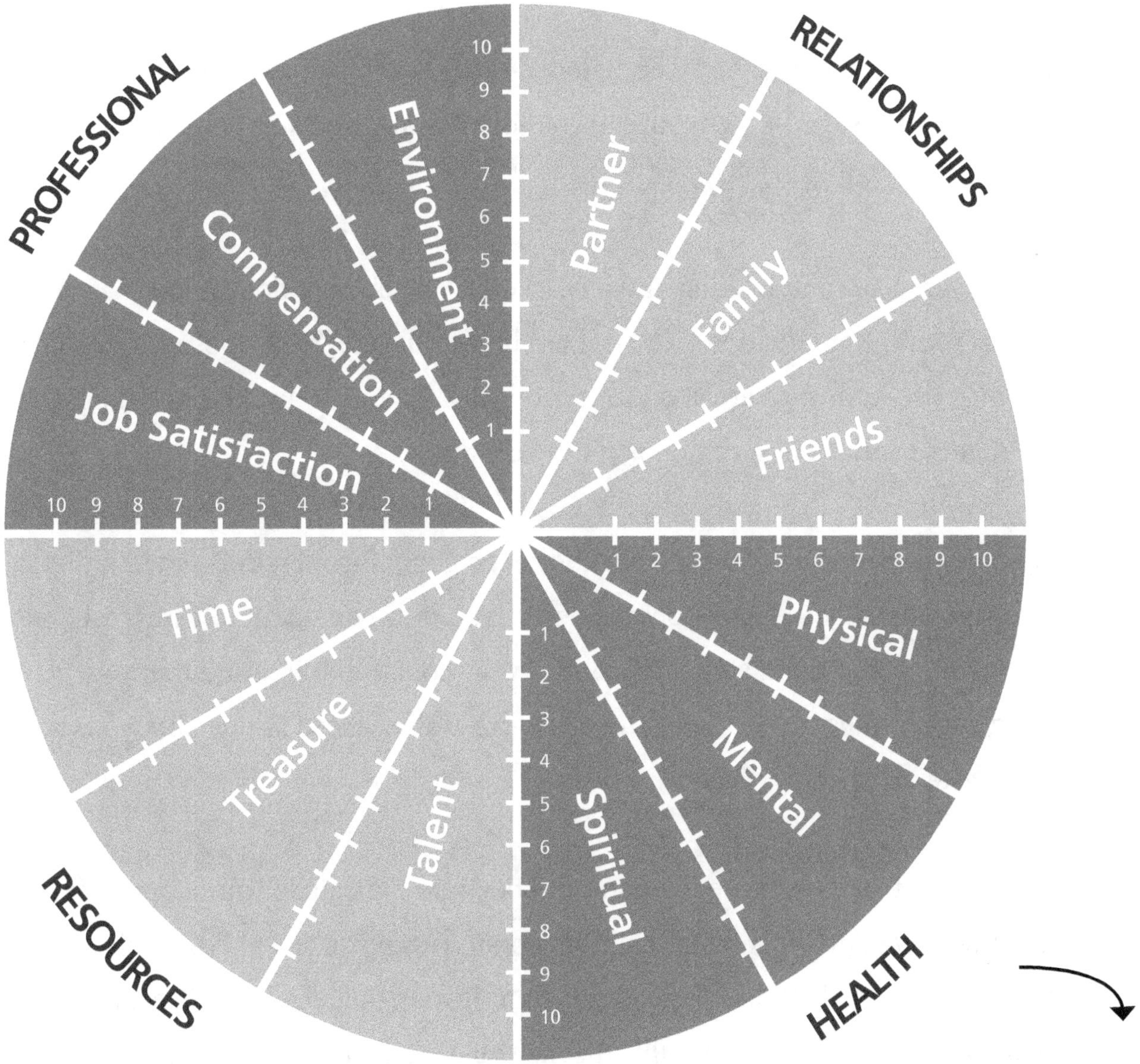

Instructions: *Use the assessment on the following two pages to calculate your average for each subsection. For each subsection in the wheel below, draw a line to match each score.*

Example: $\dfrac{9 + 7 + 3 + 6 + 5}{\text{Each Question's Score}}$ = $\dfrac{30}{\text{Total Physical Score}}$ ÷ $\dfrac{5}{\text{\# of Questions}}$ = $\dfrac{6}{\text{Subsection Average}}$

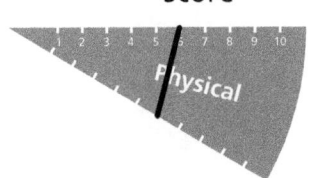

37

CONCLUSION

Now that you have completed The Balance Wheel exercise, we will explore what your results may suggest. I encourage you to write any notes or conclusions you come to on the following page.

Taking a step back and looking at your Balance Wheel, how does it look? Is it perfectly round, smooth, and filled out all the way around? Or does it have some flat spots (also known as areas of opportunities)? Since we are human beings, it is likely that the second description is more accurate.

Remember to pat yourself on the back for even going through this and defining where you currently are; most people don't. You now can begin to assess where you want to go and build a plan to achieve your goal. Keep in mind that you probably will not be able to immediately address all of these issues...but you can certainly start!

Areas with flat spots indicate low scores. They also indicate learning opportunities. Ask yourself what it will take for each section to reach a score of '10'. Think about what "great" could look like for each section. If your Balance Wheel sections are equally filled out, good for you; this means you are strong in these areas. Think about what you could do to make them even better.

When you start looking at life through the lens of strengths and opportunities, you begin seeing things in a very different light.

CONCLUSION NOTES

PART II:
VISUALIZE

VISUALIZE INTRODUCTION

In sports, a great coach inspires their team to visualize success. When each member begins to visualize and feels like they are working in sync with their team, success is possible. The ball goes in the hoop every time. The crowd goes crazy in support. That rush of euphoria from winning the championship. **Magic happens!**

The reality is every team can't win every game and the championship. However, I believe that the team that visualizes success early and works toward that goal will have a much better shot at securing the trophy than other teams.

Visualization is the process of creating an image in your brain of the desired outcome you want to achieve. The more specific and real you can make it, the better. Think of this as a way of recruiting your subconscious to help you reach your dreams.

When I lead people through this exercise, I instruct them to get as specific as possible. Set a date or timeframe during which you will achieve this outcome then begin to fill in the specifics. These specifics should include how you feel, and the impacts of these outcomes on you and those around you. In some cases, we get as granular as specific colors and smells associated with the outcomes.

Dream boards or vision boards are another way to visualize future outcomes with pictures. A dream board is a collage of images and words that reflect your goals and/or the people who will be impacted by these outcomes. It is important to put your dream board in a location where you will see it often to remind you of your goals and direction. I have one set up on the back of my home office door.

For the skeptics, this is not just pixie dust; there is actually science backing the benefits of visualization. Our subconscious is amazing. Visualizing is a way of engaging our subconscious to help us achieve our outcomes. As author William Arthur Ward said, "If you can imagine it, you can achieve it." The more you visualize the outcome, the more you will actually experience the emotions associated with the outcome. This feeling may create a bit of stress and contradiction between where you are and where you want to be. Because of this tension, your subconscious begins to strongly influence the direction and decisions you make. These decisions drive actions; as a result, there is an increased likelihood that you will make good choices that lead to the desired outcome – the outcome you originally visualized.

A personal example of this was my first ultra-marathon. I visualized crossing the finish line before the cut-off, smiling, and feeling great. I imagined the sun on my face, the hug from my wife, and the overwhelming feeling of accomplishment. It worked! I started that visualization almost a year before the race. I know that having that visualization, while overweight and sitting on the couch, helped to drive the decisions and direction for my training. Those decisions included losing weight, hiring a great endurance coach, showing up for unending workouts (sometimes at 4:00 a.m.), having a better diet, and so on. All of these actions were influenced by my subconscious because I had clearly visualized it.

The work and staying on track became much easier because my subconscious was steering me to make the right decisions. The visualization was the starting point and the major influencer. From there, I just had to break it down and do the work.

I guide leaderships teams through a similar exercise, and I can tell you that it is a repeated success. The key is to dream as big as you can while still fully buying into the idea that even if it is outrageous, it is still possible.

I can hear some of you saying, "Visualize? I have never done anything like that before in my life. How can I do this?" I suggest that we visualize all the time, though typically in the short term. So, we know how; we simply need to adjust our vision and dream bigger.

Here is an example of how we visualize every day. When you are driving your car, you are visualizing. Let's say you are at a stoplight, waiting for the light to change. You visualize that when the light turns green, you will confirm it is safe to go, press on the accelerator, and begin moving through the intersection. After you have been driving for any length of time, your subconscious takes over this process for you. When you are first learning to drive, however, you likely went through a visualization process to make it happen. **Whether it is a traffic light or an ultra-marathon, visualization works.**

EXERCISE: VISUALIZATION

The intention of the next exercise is to begin identifying where you want to go with regards to each quadrant of The Balance Wheel. When you break down your visualizations into different segments, it often becomes much easier to define what great looks like for a particular section.

On the following pages, list out (in bullet points) what great looks like for you within each quadrant. I encourage you to review every section of The Balance Wheel and ask yourself what would life have to look like for it to rank a '10'? When you reach an answer, write it out. Also, write down what it will feel like to achieve that outcome. Go through each point and make a couple of notes in the corresponding quadrant.

There is an example at the start of each quadrant on the following pages to help you get started.

PROFESSIONAL

YOUR JOB TITLE AND HOW MUCH YOU ARE EARNING.

Example: • *I'm excited to get out of bed every morning and go to work. I love the work that I do and the people that I work with. I know my work has meaning, and I'm excited for my professional career.*

PART II: VISUALIZE

RESOURCES

THE TYPE OF CAR YOU DRIVE AND ONE SPECIAL SPLURGE.

Example: • *I feel in control of my finances and my time. I'm living well within my means. I'm building and saving for my future. I'm planning on buying my tiny house and taking two months off a year for adventure.*

RELATIONSHIPS

BE SPECIFIC ABOUT WHO YOU SEE YOURSELF WITH AND HOW IT FEELS.

Example: • *I am in a supportive and loving relationship. I am excited for our future. I have valuable friends that I see on a regular basis, and I spend quality time with my family.*

HEALTH

IF YOU ARE LOOKING TO LOSE WEIGHT, WRITE DOWN YOUR TARGET WEIGHT. IF YOU WANT TO COMPLETE A SPECIFIC EVENT, WRITE IT DOWN. IF IT INVOLVES YOUR CHURCH OR FAITH, WRITE IT DOWN AND OWN IT.

Example: • *I am in the best physical, mental, and spiritual health in my life. I have completed three ultra-marathons with plans for more. I sleep well at night and have no fears of the future.*

CONCLUSION

Congratulations! You are joining a small group of people who choose to live their lives proactively, not reactively. You may feel that nothing has changed, but you are starting to define what great looks like holistically and for you, on your terms. Most people live their entire lives reacting to what comes along. You have now partnered with your subconscious.

The intention of The Balance Wheel exercise is to empower you to think differently and holistically about success. I encourage you to review your four visualizations and look for any themes or commonalities. Are there any items that must first be achieved in order for you to achieve the other items? In some cases, this may not be the most fun item on the list, but it is critical to complete before you move on to the next task. Often, knowing the great things that will follow empowers us to get through something we had been avoiding up until that point.

If you view these challenging hurdles as simply starting points, they will become easier to achieve. As an example, if you have visualized an amazing career in a field you are not currently in, please do not feel defeated by this. It reaffirms to me it is likely the right direction, although you may face some hurdles around education or training.

For Reka, when she visualized changing careers from that of an accountant to a therapist and coach, she encountered tons of hurdles. It did not matter - she had visualized where she wanted to go and made it happen. The return to school, the certification, and a new culture were all just hurdles.

These visualizations will be critical in helping you achieve those goals.

Helping people who want to transition to building their own business is one of the areas in which I specialize. If you are interested in this, *The Aspiring Solopreneur: Your Business Start-Up Bible* may be for you.

You can learn more at **www.hippycapitalist.com.**

PART III:
LIFE-CHANGING GOAL (LCG)

*"If you don't know where you are going,
any road will get you there."*

– Lewis Carroll, author of *Alice's Adventures in Wonderland*

LIFE-CHANGING GOAL (LCG) INTRODUCTION

Few people realize their potential. I believe the main reason this happens is due to our tendency to lose sight of where we want to go, or because we have not clearly defined what we want in life. As a result, many individuals drift through their entire. Mediocrity reins and "Good enough" becomes the norm.

I do not agree with this. "Good enough" sucks!

It is okay to want more, and it is okay to be amazing.

The challenge is that so many of us know we want more, but have no idea how to define or achieve it. I suggest that there is little training and almost no formal education that teaches you how to dream big. In spite of this, it is still your personal obligation to figure it out. The person you see in the mirror is 100% accountable for where you are in life today - the good and the bad. Life may have thrown you some curveballs, which is okay and normal. We have all been there, so own it! Embrace the idea that what you can achieve is limited only by your own thinking. Instead of allowing the curveballs to define you, let them motivate you to become more.

I like to say, **"Extraordinary lives in the unreasonable, so be unreasonable."**

Contrary to the modern media spin, we live in some of the most abundant times ever. In virtually every means used to calculate human abundance as a society, we are thriving. These include health, literacy, life expectancy, infant mortality rate, education, wealth, food production, the number of trees, communication, connectedness, and so on. As humans, we are kicking ass. There are plenty of opportunities, and I believe things are only going to get better.

With this current abundance comes the unique challenge of defining what we want. For many around the globe they may be the first generation that doesn't have to invest most of their time simply surviving. Most of us no longer have to stay solely focused on finding enough food and clean water or avoiding bad guys or chopping firewood. As a result, we have an abundance of time. This is an opportunity to step back and think about what we want. Thinking intently about what we want can be scary. It can also be incredibly empowering.

The Balance Wheel is intended to build awareness of where you are today and to empower you to see future opportunities for growth. Visualizing helps you dream to see what amazing looks like on a holistic level. This next exercise, the Life-Changing Goal, or LCG, is designed to narrow your focus to one specific target or to identify directional themes. Once armed with a clear destination, the path to get there will start materializing.

Studies indicate businesses that consistently outperform their competitors have clear, simple, long-term, and enormous goals. Jim Collins, the author of *Built to Last: Successful Habits of Visionary Companies*[3], calls these "Big Hairy Audacious Goals" (BHAG). I have seen firsthand how impactful this concept works in both business and personal life.

EXERCISE: IMAGINE YOUR LCG

The intention of the LCG exercise is to identify different ways of dreaming, learn how to narrow things down, and define where you want to go.

Read through the following three prompts and write your responses below each one.

Prompt #1: Imagine you just won the lottery. Sit back and visualize it in your head. See yourself holding a $200 million check. After taxes, you can still afford almost anything imaginable. Maybe it looks like a dream cruise around Europe, starting your own business, owning a Ferrari, or going back to school. Perhaps it means you pay for a dozen college tuitions or start a non-profit llama rescue (yeah, that last one may sound crazy, but think outside the box). Remember, these are your dreams – be unreasonable!

In the blanks below, write the top five things you would do with your newfound wealth.

1. _____

2. _____

3. _____

4. _____

5. _____

Prompt #2: For this prompt, let's say that your long-lost, eccentric aunt just passed. Even though you did not know each other very well, she left you a yearly allowance that is twice your current income. Although it is great money, it comes with a catch: you must be learning or pursuing something you love. In other words, you have all the time in the world, but you have to be working towards a dream or improving yourself. This may involve finding your dream job, returning to school, writing a book, getting physically fit, running a triathlon, or helping others in some form. Again, this is your opportunity to dream about what you would do if you had all the time in the world.

Below, write the top five things you would do if you had unlimited time.

1. _____

2. _____

3. _____

4. _____

5. _____

Prompt #3: For our last prompt, visualize being at the doctor's office. He has good news and bad news for you. The good news is, currently, you are healthy. The bad news is the doctor found an aneurysm and he knows, with certainty, that you will die in exactly three years and one day (FYI, no doctor can actually do this). The point is this: you now have an expiration date. Think about what you would do if you had just received this information. What would you do if you knew you had a specific expiration date? Maybe you would go heli-skiing, visit every national park in the country, teach people to dance, write a memoir, move closer to family, or make an impactful difference in some way.

Below, write the top five things you would do with your remaining time.

1. _____

2. _____

3. _____

4. _____

5. _____

PART III: LIFE-CHANGING GOAL (LCG)

EXERCISE: NARROW TO ONE

Once you have five answers listed per prompt, write them all in the blanks below. Duplicate items should only be listed once.

1. _____
2. _____
3. _____
4. _____
5. _____
6. _____
7. _____
8. _____
9. _____
10. _____
11. _____
12. _____
13. _____
14. _____
15. _____

From here, compare each item, one at a time by asking yourself, "Would I rather do #1 (take a cruise around Europe) or #2 (start my own business)?" Put a tick mark next to your preference. Compare #1 with #3, and check your preference. Continue comparing #1 with each item on the list and mark your preferences. Repeat this process with #2 and #3, putting a tick mark next to your preference. Next, compare #2 with #4, then #2 with #5, and so on. Repeat this process until all numbers have been compared to one another and your preferences have been marked.

Now that you have completed the narrowing process, count the number of tick marks next to each number.

It is at this point where I have seen folks realize they have rekindled a long-lost childhood dream that was once crushed by an authority figure. In other cases, people begin noticing a theme around the top several items. I have also witnessed this exercise bring to life an unknown desire to try something completely new. The first time Reka did this exercise, she determined she wanted to do a wilderness survival course within one year (I did *not* see that one coming!). But it is her LCG, not mine. As a Londoner/city girl, this was a big deal for Reka. She researched and took a course, which helped empower her in many aspects of life. It was a great step for her confidence that enabled her to take on bigger challenges.

Keep in mind that it is okay if your LCG involves a big house, money, or stuff. This is your life! It does not matter what others think.

While working on narrowing it down to one item, you may not have a clear outcome. If this is the case, look for common themes in the top few items and work from there. See if you can find something that will pull them together in a simple way.

When I completed this exercise years ago, I did not have a crystal-clear, singular item at the top. I realized that the top four items involved helping others and having a positive impact. **With this thinking in mind, I created the LCG I have today:**

By July 16th, 2027, I will have introduced one million people to a new way of thinking, and will impact 100,000 lives for the better.

Big and scary! I literally struggled with putting my pen to paper when I first wrote this. Who was I to be so audacious? How could I do something so big? What the hell was I thinking? I kicked all those thoughts to the curb and wrote it out.

You do not have to know exactly how you will reach your LCG - that will come.

If you completed this exercise and feel this whole thing fell flat, please be patient with yourself. Sometimes, there are bright lightbulb moments and other times, there are none. It is all perfectly normal and okay! Believe it or not, the simple act of going through this exercise will help your subconscious start the process of clarifying what you want. If needed, go back and review your visualizations to look for any unifying themes. Let it sit for a week then come back and review. You may be surprised at what bubbles up.

In a few cases, I have noticed that people end up with two different LCGs. This may be in separate areas of influence, such as health and employment. This is also okay. Try combining them to clarify your direction. Perhaps your LCG involves changing careers, landing your dream job, doing something completely different, or simply gaining employment, given the current pandemic situation. I believe that when you are defining where you want to go in life, that dream must include alignment with your job or career.

You are discovering why you do what you do. This is a cornerstone in finding work you will love and in achieving a happy, fulfilled life.

For this section, if what you came up with as your LCG does not involve your career or a job, don't worry about it – it seldom does! We will specifically address the job later.

PART III: LIFE-CHANGING GOAL (LCG)

EXERCISE: IDENTIFY YOUR LCG

Now that you are narrowing in on the direction you want to go, it is time to put a completion date on it. Write down when you will achieve your LCG using specific terms. You will want to be able to remember it going forward.

I like to take this a step further by making it into an affirmation statement. I suggest starting with the phrase "I will...by [the date defined]." By setting a date and turning it into an affirmative, we are recruiting our subconscious to make this dream a reality.

For my achievement date, I chose my 60th birthday. I know that setting a date will help my subconscious lead me in making the right decisions that ultimately result in me achieving the desired outcome. If you are looking to change careers, this date may be several years away. If you are searching for a new dream job, it may only be a few months out...or sooner.

Write out when you will achieve your LCG and what, specifically, you will see.

I WILL...

_____

_____

_____

_____

_____

BY: _____

DATE: _____

NEXT STEPS

Now that you have assessed where you are today, visualized where you want to go in the future, and narrowed your dreams into an LCG, it is time to break it all down. It may seem like a lot of information to organize and process, so try keeping this old adage in mind:

How do you eat an elephant?
Answer: One bite at a time.

On the following pages, list out everything you will need to do to achieve your LCG. It is okay if the list is long. Be specific.

For example, when I started doing endurance events, I knew I needed to lose weight. I listed it out. I knew that I needed to learn about nutrition, so I added that. I knew I would need a coach to teach me how to exercise without hurting myself, so I wrote that down, too.

Knowing the steps needed to achieve your LCG is important in defining alignment with the right type of work and job you will be pursuing. **We will do a similar process for helping you identify and achieve your ideal job. We will talk about these in more detail later.**

PART III: LIFE-CHANGING GOAL (LCG)

EXERCISE: WHAT NEEDS TO BE DONE?

In the blanks below, list out everything that needs to be done in order for you to achieve your LCG.

1. Complete this workbook
2.
3.
4.
5.
6.
7.
8.
9.
10.
11.
12.
13.
14.
15.
16.
17.
18.
19.
20.
21.
22.
23.
24.
25.
26.
27.
28.
29.
30.
31.
32.
33.
34.
35.
36.
37.
38.
39.
40.

EXERCISE: NARROW IT DOWN

Well done! Next, go through all the items and look for the first things that must happen for you to achieve your LCG. Review the list and be honest with yourself. Keep drilling down and narrowing that focus until you have identified the three most critical items to complete first.

An example of this might be around an LCG that requires some finances, and you are currently cash-strapped and living paycheck to paycheck. This is when it is important to be honest and pragmatic, as you may have to make difficult changes to achieve your LCG. If you are currently broke and looking to change your situation, the first three items listed may look like this:

1. **Read** a book on personal budgeting and finance.
2. **Build** a personal budget and identify three ways to save money.
3. **Open** a separate savings account for your LCG.

In the spaces below, write the first three things from your long list that you need to do to get this rolling. Assign a completion date for each item. Make sure the date is no further out than 30 days. If it is, it is too big of a step.

Item #1: _____ Date: _____

Item #2: _____ Date: _____

Item #3: _____ Date: _____

PART III: LIFE-CHANGING GOAL (LCG)

YOUR IDEAL JOB

I imagine some of you might be saying, "Okay, this is great. I want to be proactive in my life, but I am currently out of work. This book was supposed to help me find a job. What does any of this have to do with getting a job?" I would argue, everything.

Right now, your LCG may not have anything to do with a job, career, or work environment. The critical thing is start defining where you are going, what is important to you, and to learn the mechanics of figuring out how to get there - which is what you have been doing so far.

Remember the statistic suggesting 85% of people hate their jobs? Each exercise you have completed so far will help clarify what great looks like for you and on your terms. Your job also needs to be in alignment with this thinking. Knowing what you want will assist your search for a dream job that provides you time, talent, and treasure to achieve these dreams. If your LCG involves your career or job, even better.

If you are unemployed, you have the opportunity to find your ideal fit. If you are underemployed or miserably employed, that is not your boss's fault; it is yours for staying. To be clear, I am not saying we can all quit our jobs tomorrow. In fact, very few of us can comfortably do that. However, I am saying that if you know what is important in your life and where you want to go, you can begin making a plan to change your current life situation and build your intentional life. Again, this may not happen tomorrow, but you are starting the process.

So, if you are reading this and you find yourself as an unemployed COVID-19 work refugee, I congratulate you. You can now begin building your dream life.

Armed with this new awareness, vision, LCG direction, and the freedom to look for your next gig, you can proactively search for the type of work that will be aligned with these values and goals.

WHAT IS YOUR DREAM JOB?

Take a few minutes to write how your ideal workday would look today. Be specific. Think about how far away the ideal work environment is from your home. Could you ride a bike to work, or are you driving a brand-new car? Is the company large or small? Is it uptight or casual? Will you have friends there? Do you take your lunch hour to exercise? What will your boss be like? What sort of compensation are you getting? How aligned is this new job with your Balance Wheel, vision, and LCG? Will this new job provide the resources, time, and finances needed to achieve your dream life? What does it feel like to come home happy at the end of a great workday, and to be enthusiastic to return the next day? Your subconscious helps drive the decisions you make to ensure this vision becomes a reality.

Because you are building your ideal life, you may be turning everything upside down with this vision. Perhaps your dream is to ride your bike to work on country roads, but today, you live in the city. This means you may need to consider relocating. If you dreamed of driving a new car, but are buried in school debt, you may have to simplify your life and get out of debt. Each of these factors will contribute to your job needs, as well as your happiness.

If you truly want those things, or anything for that matter, that is great! It does not matter what kind of situation you are in now because you can change it. **Mindset matters – and as soon as you see where you want to go, you can start taking steps towards living your ideal life.**

EXERCISE: VISUALIZE YOUR DREAM JOB

In the spaces below, describe a visualization of what your ideal job looks like. Remember to be specific and to include other aspects of your life that will be impacted.

_____
_____
_____
_____
_____
_____
_____
_____
_____
_____
_____

When working with coaching senior executives in transition, I consistently push to start with these processes first. I believe a vision of a well-balanced life dramatically impacts the job search and interview processes. When a person looks for a new job, they typically focus on pay, title, and vacation time; however, most end up hating their jobs for completely different reasons. Starting with an aligned, holistic vision will set the stage for finding the right opportunities.

Remember, we are playing the long game here. Depending on what you are building and your situation, several steps may be involved, which is okay. **Take it one step at a time and stay focused on manifesting your ideal life. You will get there!**

PART IV:
MAKE IT HAPPEN

WHO CAN HELP? INTRODUCTION

Most human beings are hard-wired to help others. When an individual approaches me wanting to sell something, my guard goes up. If the same person asks for help, I would likely do what I could to assist – even if the actions they are requesting are the same, but with different approaches. An excellent way to begin the job hunt is to find folks who are currently employed in a field of expertise that interests you. Look for people who seem happy or like where they work. You can probably learn something from them. From there, start talking with these people to educate yourself on why they are happy.

When you start meeting with folks, simply talk with them and learn why they are happy. If it is because they love where they work, ask if they are hiring. Even if they are not hiring, ask if you could speak with anyone at that company who loves their job. Be proactive and learn as much as you can.

Think about all the people you know. Begin narrowing it down to the folks who work in or near the same area of expertise as you, who seem to love their companies, or who work in organizations that can use your skills. List out these people then go back and identify who you think may share similar beliefs or values as you. These can be diverse and wide-ranging. For example, if you are a family-oriented person, look for someone who also values family time. If you like fancy cars and big houses, find that person on your list. If you want to attend every one of your daughter's soccer games, who on your list is also doing that?

List these people and companies on the following pages.

PART IV: MAKE IT HAPPEN

SAME AREA OF EXPERTISE

1. _____
2. _____
3. _____
4. _____
5. _____
6. _____
7. _____
8. _____
9. _____
10. _____
11. _____
12. _____
13. _____
14. _____
15. _____

SIMILAR BELIEFS

1. _____
2. _____
3. _____
4. _____
5. _____
6. _____
7. _____
8. _____
9. _____
10. _____
11. _____
12. _____
13. _____
14. _____
15. _____

WHAT TO ASK?

Now that you have a list of people and companies, it is time to reach out to them. Try not to overthink this. All you need to do is start a conversation. Ask simple, open-ended questions to get the job search rolling. It may sound something like this:

> "Hi, Jane. Thank you for taking my call. I am hoping to get some advice. I am currently on the hunt for a new position with an organization that shares my values. It appears you are pretty happy with where you work. If you were in my shoes, where would you be looking for work these days?"

Perhaps there is an available position there – who knows? Now, sit back, listen, and take notes. When the conversation slows down, ask a few more questions, such as:

1. **"Is there anyone [at a different company that you like and think I would fit in] that you could connect me with?"**
2. **"What other companies to do you like that engage in a similar business?"**
3. **"Is there anyone else you suggest I speak with?"**
4. **"What else should I be asking that I am not?"**

You never know where these conversations will go, so stay focused and on your toes. Remember to be respectful of their time. An old school handwritten Thank You note never hurts, either. They may not have an opening today, but you never know about tomorrow. The goal is to find a possible referral in a place that is a great fit or to begin identifying companies are in alignment with your values and beliefs.

You can still use the traditional sources like online job boards or recruiters for finding open jobs. **However, before submitting an application, I encourage you to research each company and determine if they would be a good fit.**

QUESTIONS TO ASK

QUESTIONS TO ASK

INTERVIEWING

Once you have found a few places to interview, it is time to prepare to interview them. Finding the right fit for you is 100% critical. I define 'fit' as "sharing similar beliefs, values, skills, and expectations". Start asking yourself questions such as: *Is this a place I will love going to every day? Does it involve the type of work I love doing? Do I like these people?* This is what the interview process should be about. If you find an organization that is offering great compensation, but does not share your values, they are not a good fit. In this situation, I suggest you run away. Even if the money is great, but you do not fit, you will likely become miserable and things will go downhill from there. You will be back among the 85% that hate their job.

Interviews are your opportunity to learn about the company and for the company to learn about you. Try to embrace a spirit of curiosity by remembering the interview process is a two-way street. They may want you, or you might not like them. Either way, it is a win because you avoided future challenges you were bound to run into.

Based on The Balance Wheel, visualizations, and the LCG exercise, begin building a list of questions that will allow you to learn and interview the company based on your need for fit. This will enhance the likelihood of you achieving success on your terms.

HERE ARE SOME EXAMPLES OF QUESTIONS TO ASK DURING AN INTERVIEW:

1. "My family time is important. I am happy to occasionally do a little more work from home, but I want to make sure I can be home for family dinner every night at 6:00. Will that be possible?"

2. "I am working on my fitness and noticed there is a gym here. When is it open, is there any training, and how often can I use it?"

3. "I enjoy doing what I do, but I want to go back to school part-time. Does your company offer any tuition or training reimbursement?"

4. "My budget is a little tight right now. I am happy to work evenings and weekends for overtime. What kind of overtime compensation do you offer?"

5. "I like to get acquainted with my coworkers on a personal level. Are there any company sports or events?"

6. "I like knowing where I stand with my direct boss. Is there any way I can speak with him/her to see how we would fit working together?"

7. "What are the growth opportunities within the company and how long does it usually take?"

8. "Do the employee benefits cover my family; if not, what is the cost for me?"

9. "If you were in my shoes, what other questions should I be asking that I am not?"

These are just a few examples of how you can evaluate the company during your job interview to determine if it is a good mutual fit. Sometimes, you may not be able to find your ideal fit; so, think about what you are willing to accept as temporary tradeoffs. I believe these tradeoffs are much easier to do when we have a long-term goal in mind. This can make challenging jobs tolerable because we know there is a reason behind *why* we are doing what we are doing.

I can remember when I was 19 years old. I had a miserable job that paid very well, but it was a nightmare. I hated it. If I had to work there for a long time, I would not have lasted a week. I knew I was going to be there for a matter of months and the money I earned was going to help me out of a jam. This made the decision to suck it up and keep working easier because I knew it was not forever. It was a means to an end.

Looking ahead, try to avoid this means-to-an end thinking. Ideally, search for positions where you would be a great fit and where the job aligns with your visualization and LCG. Finding this fit will make a job much more enjoyable, which will show in all aspects of your life. In the long run, you will likely make more money because we typically do better work when we are in a place we love.

As you go through the interview process, remember to ask questions and listen. Do your best to read between the lines. You are looking to see if a certain company fits with your visualization of what a great job and work environment look like. I realize that if money is really tight or if you have an extremely hard time not having any kind of job, it can be challenging to shift to a different mindset. However, if you want to find your ideal job, it is critical to do so. **Take your time, be proactive, and keep hunting for the right fit.**

MY INTERVIEW QUESTIONS

MY INTERVIEW QUESTIONS

PART IV: MAKE IT HAPPEN

ACTION ITEMS

Reading a book and changing your thinking is a monumental start. Making sure you actually do the work, like researching, making calls, and following up, is just as important.

In Part III, you listed out everything that needed to be done to achieve your LCG. You are refining the process of thinking holistically and identifying all the pieces. You will need to do the same thing here to obtain your ideal job. Will you need to improve your skills? Are you considering relocating? Do you need to simplify your lifestyle? How will you get started? Think about who you will need to call, which job posting platforms you should check daily, and which companies to research. This is an opportune time to update your resume, buy Thank You cards, speak with recruiters, or update your LinkedIn status.

Take some time to think about your ideal job and everything it will take to land it.

On the next few pages, write down all the items that come to mind.

UNEMPLOYED?

WHAT NEEDS TO BE DONE...

TO OBTAIN MY DREAM JOB?

WHAT NEEDS TO BE DONE...

PART IV: MAKE IT HAPPEN

TO OBTAIN MY DREAM JOB?

Over time, you will knock things off the list and add to it – that is fine. The intention is that you have a centralized place to use as a short-term parking lot of items that need to be done, as well as opportunities and challenges. By centralizing this list in one place, you will allow your subconscious to know that nothing is falling through the cracks. Keep adding things here so you do not have to spend any energy on them until you are ready to dive in and focus on the task at hand.

Now that you have built this list, it is time to get focused. Just as we narrowed the action items around achieving your LCG in Part III, we will do something similar here: a monthly review. You will use your big list of action items for getting a job then filter them down to which tasks need to be completed daily.

Review the entire list of what needs to be done to obtain your ideal job. Consider the top five critical things to get started. List these out below.

1. _____

2. _____

3. _____

4. _____

5. _____

Stay focused on these five things and only these five things; you will be much more productive and efficient. Keep working on them and crossing them off when they are done. When you have completed all five items, go back to determine the next five most critical items. Remember that they need to be critical tasks – not easy, fun, or things you have already done.

Here is an example:

1. **Finalize my visualization of what a great job looks like and write it out.**
2. **Finalize my list of people who I believe like their jobs.**
3. **Identify five online resources to check daily for job postings.**
4. **Update my resume.**
5. **Finalize my list of questions to ask people who like their jobs.**

Once these have been completed, the next five items may look like the following:

1. **Review my ideal job visualization and write out additional skills I will need.**
2. **Check all job posting resources.**
3. **Buy Thank You notes.**
4. **Review and practice the questions to ask the interviewer.**
5. **Call five people at companies I like and ask my questions.**

After these items are done, go back and review the entire list then come up with the next list of action items that needs to be addressed. Most likely, as you go through the process, new action items will arise from each step. List those in your parking lot of things that need to be addressed. Keep repeating this focused process and you will achieve more than you can imagine.

5 STEPS AT A TIME

1. _____
2. _____
3. _____
4. _____
5. _____

1. _____
2. _____
3. _____
4. _____
5. _____

1. _____
2. _____
3. _____
4. _____
5. _____

PART IV: MAKE IT HAPPEN

5 STEPS AT A TIME

1. _____
2. _____
3. _____
4. _____
5. _____

1. _____
2. _____
3. _____
4. _____
5. _____

1. _____
2. _____
3. _____
4. _____
5. _____

UNEMPLOYED?

5 STEPS AT A TIME

1. _____
2. _____
3. _____
4. _____
5. _____

1. _____
2. _____
3. _____
4. _____
5. _____

1. _____
2. _____
3. _____
4. _____
5. _____

5 STEPS AT A TIME

1. _____
2. _____
3. _____
4. _____
5. _____

1. _____
2. _____
3. _____
4. _____
5. _____

1. _____
2. _____
3. _____
4. _____
5. _____

ACCOUNTABILITY

My goal is to give you every tool, tip, and trick in the book to help you get through some of the harder stuff. You have created visualizations and defined your LCG. You have written them out and know what success looks like. You have defined your action items and started to prioritize each step. Now, how do you hold yourself accountable?

It is similar to knowing you are going to get fit. You visualize abs of steel or crossing the finish line. You know what it will take. You build your daily routine. Next, you are ready to do sit-ups, sprints, or weight training. When you are inspired, it is easy to get started. Realistically, after a week of doing sit-ups, you may hurt all over and not look any different. Remember, you are making changes – sticking with it is essential.

This is when accountability matters.

A few individuals are able to hold themselves accountable by taping pictures or notes to their bathroom mirrors, for example. This way, they see the image every day and are reminded of it, which helps to reaffirm their motivation and accountability.

I encourage you to take this process seriously, like it is your job...because it is. This means keeping a routine by consistently getting into the office early, even if "the office" is the kitchen table. Regular breaks are a good idea. Communicate with others in your household about when you will be working. Dress as if you are going to your ideal job, as this makes a difference in how you present yourself to others, even if it is only a phone call. Devote the time and energy you would as if you were working, but focus on finding your ideal fit. This is a major step towards disciplined accountability.

A significant number of people see great value in having an accountability partner. This should be someone you trust, is in a similar position, and will hold your feet to the fire. It is all about positivity, accountability, and keeping things focused and progressing in spite of setbacks.

In some cases, folks want to choose their partner or spouse. I usually recommend against this because that person may already feel nervous about their partner's current unemployment; they may push in the wrong direction or have short-sighted motivations.

Regardless of who you choose, ask them to help you stay accountable.

EXERCISE: ACCOUNTABILITY PARTNERS

To begin, review with your accountability partner all the tools you have used to reach this point, including your ideal job visualization and list of action items. This will assist your accountability partner with understanding what you have done so far to define and achieve your dream job. Some things may include:

1. **Review my Balance Wheel, visualization, and LCG. Create a visualization of what a great work environment and job looks like to me.**
2. **My vision of what a great job and work environment look like.**
3. **List the people who I think have similar values and appear happy at their workplace.**
4. **Share my entire list of action items.**
5. **List the companies where I know people are happy.**
6. **Regularly check traditional sources of jobs openings.**
7. **Write a list of questions to ask people I know.**
8. **Create my list of interview questions of a company and match it to my visualization.**
9. **Show them the short list of the first five items and let them know when it will be completed.**

Once you have an accountability partner, set specific days and times to check in. In the beginning, this could be on a daily basis. For example, a short conversation at 5:15 every evening for 10 minutes may help you stay on track. This implied social agreement will ensure you do the work you committed to, stay focused on getting it done, and move your objective forward.

PART IV: MAKE IT HAPPEN

Fill in the information in the blanks below:

My accountability partner is: _____

We will meet on (date/time): _____

If you are the accountability partner, be honest, direct, and hold the other person accountable. If they do not get it done, ask them why and what can be done to ensure it gets completed. Keep on them until they finish that task. If someone completes all their tasks for a certain time period, great! They can take on a few more items. If they get these done, they should focus on the last two until they are completed. Do not add more items first! The reason for this is it can be easy to keep adding new, easier, or more fun objectives while letting the hard ones go unfinished.

Lastly, remember to celebrate even the smallest of victories. Each piece of encouragement empowers the next step. Your job is to remind them of what great will look like and how each step gets them closer to their goal.

Personal accountability is what makes a difference. This same approach works well in achieving your LCG or anything you visualize. If you use the time to build a plan for your LCG, have at it. Just make sure you block your time for when you are doing both. If you want to work on your LCG, define how many hours you can allow. Stay focused on that, but only during your allotted time. Remember, your current job is finding your dream job.

ADDITIONAL RESOURCES

You are not alone in this journey. There are hundreds of thousands of people facing similar challenges every day. Beware of the naysayers who try to drag you down into despair. Instead, focus on finding those who will support, encourage, hold you accountable, and celebrate your success.

Celebrating living life on your terms is the purpose of the Hippy Capitalist. Welcome to the revolution.

facebook

You can join our like-minded community on Facebook:

https://rebrand.ly/hippycapitalistFB

Where we:

- Celebrate success
- Learn from each other
- Have access to exclusive tools and learning videos
- Participate in private webinars
- Offer discounts on workshops and conferences
- Provide BETA access to programs and products
- Offer community coaching

ADDITIONAL RESOURCES

TRAVEL/ADVENTURE JUNKIE?

Visit our YouTube channel (https://www.youtube.com/solopreneur-life) to celebrate living life on your terms and to submit your own videos.

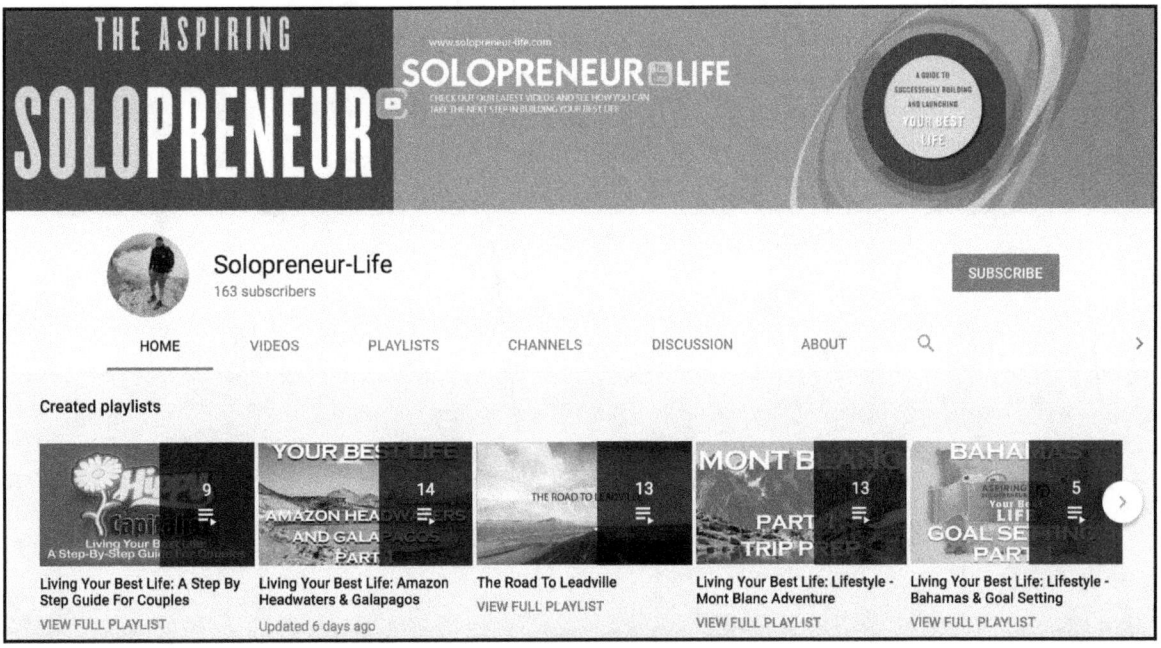

Linked in

You can also join me on LinkedIn:

https://www.linkedin.com/in/kriskluver/

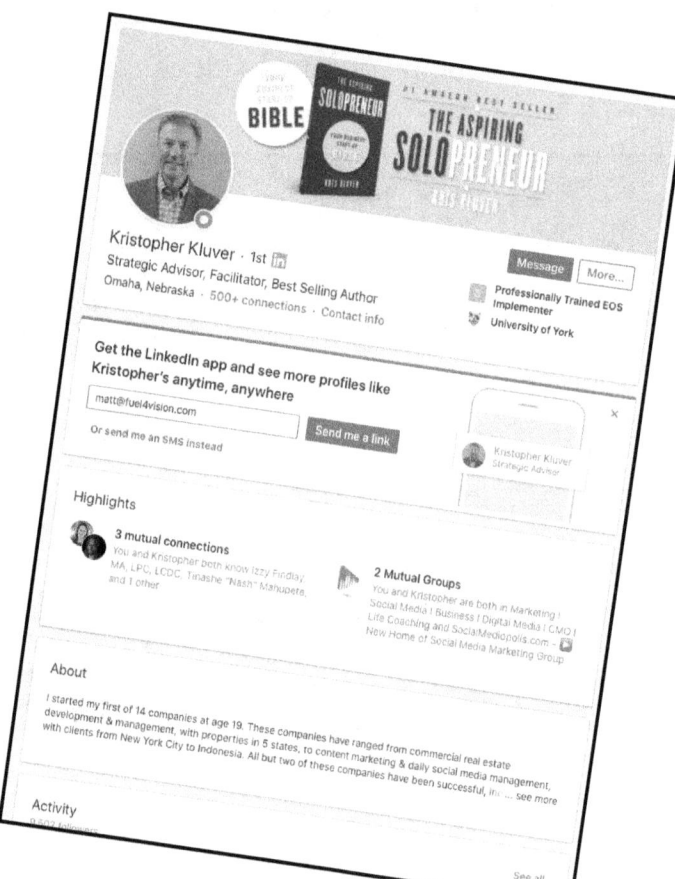

STARTING A BUSINESS?

Check out www.aspiringsolopreneur.com to gain exclusive access to many tools and resources, including:

- The Life Balance Wheel
- Delegation Matrix
- Couples retreat information
- Tri-fold template
- Defining your True North
- Defining your Why
- Life coaching

Aspiring Solopreneur Workbook | Chapter 13 | **Build Your Success Guide**

Road Map

Since you have been keeping your work together in this Workbook, you have already created your Road Map.

Take a minute to go back to the previous chapters and pull out the final outcomes from each section.

Put these documents into a separate section of your binder with the rest of the items from Chapter 13. This is your business plan! This complete plan is what you should show your advisors/lenders/your partner, and what you should reference as you launch into your solopreneur life. Clean up any documents that are messy or incomplete and we suggest getting section dividers to help organize this section because this is what you use from here on out.

Here is what you should have in your Road Map:

Chapter 1	Balance Wheel Assessment Finding Your True North Defining Your Why
Chapter 2	Life Changing Goal (LCG) Assess the Market Your Value Proposition and Niche
Chapter 5	(only one) Accountant Questions, Costs, & Time
Chapter 6	(only one) Attorney Questions, Costs, & Time
Chapter 7	(only one) Insurance Expert Questions, Costs, & Time
Chapter 8	(only one) Banker Questions, Costs, & Time
Chapter 9	(if applicable) Bank Alternative Questions, Costs, & Time
Chapter 10	(only one) Work Space Questions, Costs, & Time
Chapter 11	Marketing and Business Development Questions, Costs, & Time
Chapter 12	Government Compliance Questions, Costs, & Time

AspiringSolopreneur.com

© 2019 Charokee Street Publishing. All Rights Reserved.

ADDITIONAL RESOURCES

Aspiring Solopreneur Workbook | Chapter 13 | Build Your Success Guide

Financial Viability

Need to Haves:　　　　　　　　　　　　　　　　**Startup Costs:**　**Monthly Costs:**

　

　

　

　

　

　　　　　　　　　　　　　　　　　　　　　Totals:

Should Haves:　　　　　　　　　　　　　　　　**Startup Costs:**　**Monthly Costs:**

　

　

　

　

　

　　　　　　　　　　　　　　　　　　　　　Totals:

AspiringSolopreneur.com

© 2019 Charokee Street Publishing. All Rights Reserved.

COUPLES ONLINE WORKSHOPS AND RETREATS

Please visit **www.hippycapitalist.com** for more information on our couples online workshops and retreats.

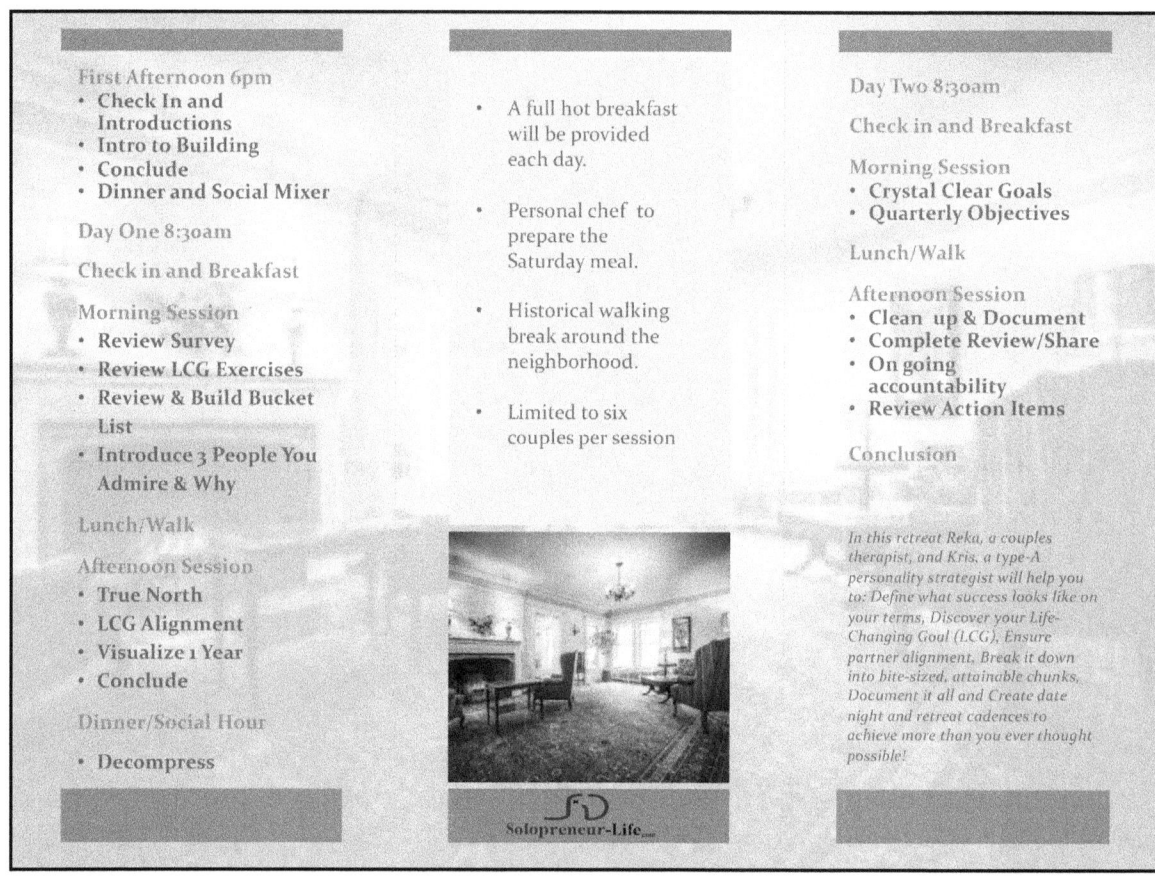

ADDITIONAL RESOURCES

SENIOR EXECS AND BUSINESS OWNERS

"LIFE ON YOUR TERMS"

6 month facilitated discovery program.

To learn more reach out to us here **www.hippycapitalist.com.**

LIFE BALANCE WHEEL

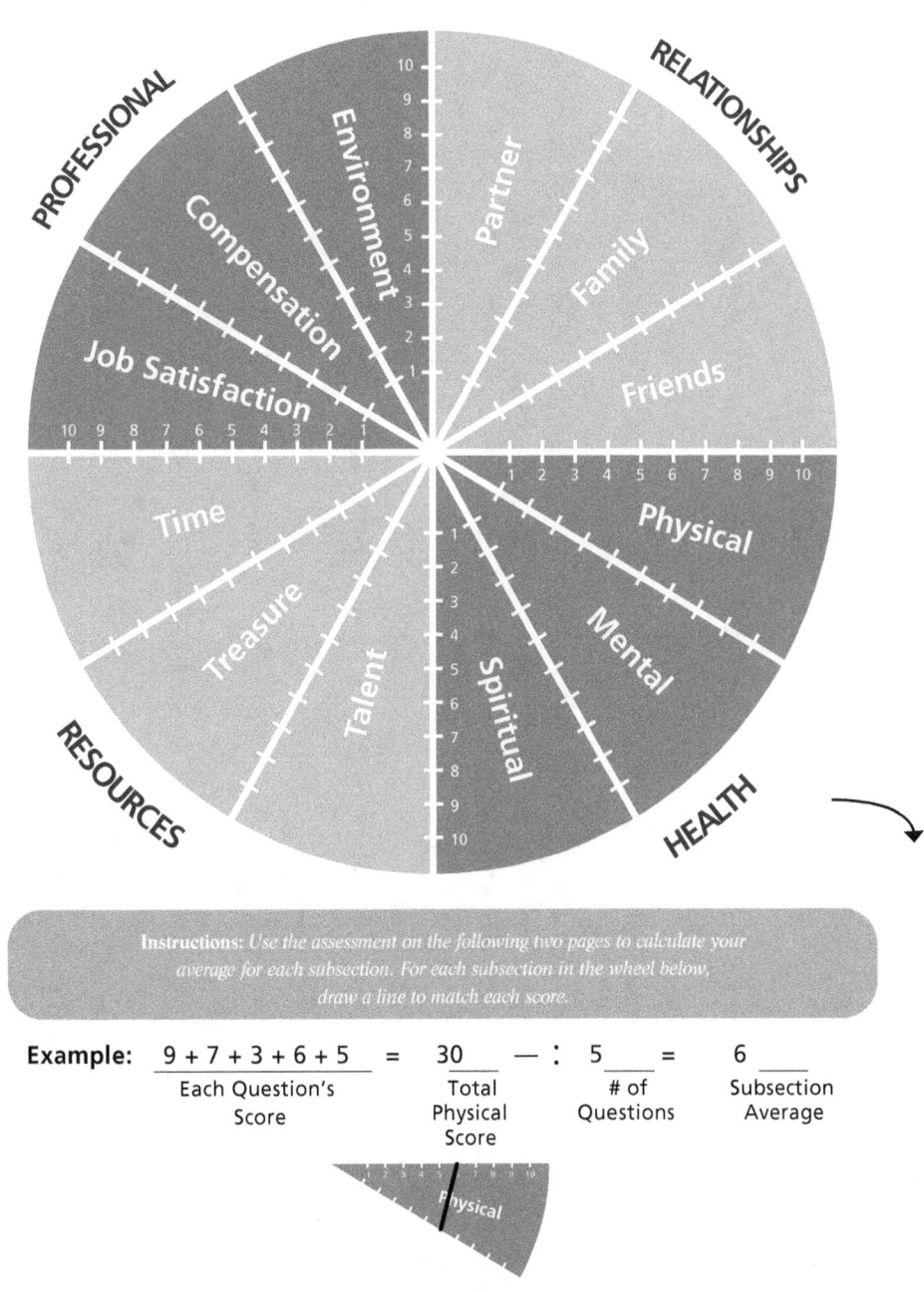

Instructions: *Use the assessment on the following two pages to calculate your average for each subsection. For each subsection in the wheel below, draw a line to match each score.*

Example: $\underbrace{9 + 7 + 3 + 6 + 5}_{\text{Each Question's Score}} = \underbrace{30}_{\substack{\text{Total} \\ \text{Physical} \\ \text{Score}}} \div \underbrace{5}_{\substack{\text{# of} \\ \text{Questions}}} = \underbrace{6}_{\substack{\text{Subsection} \\ \text{Average}}}$

CONCLUSION

I started this book with the genuine, positive intention of wishing you congratulations on being unemployed. I believe it is a wonderful opportunity to go on a treasure hunt to find your ideal job, work environment, and life. It is my heartfelt desire that you feel the same way.

You now have the tools to expand your self-awareness. You have defined areas of strengths and opportunities for growth. You can harness the power of your subconscious through visualization. Armed with this holistic knowledge, you are able to define and document what your ideal work environment and job will look like, as well as create a visualization to drive this success. You have been introduced to the processes that, when combined with a clear vision and accountable activities, will ensure you find a great work environment where you will thrive.

Congratulations and enjoy the treasure hunt for your dream job!

Once you reach your dream, I encourage you to continue using these techniques and tools, as this thinking can be channeled in many different aspects of your life.

Please share these ideas and this new way of thinking with others in your life, such as a partner, children, friends, or anyone who is looking for more. I believe there is no greater gift to give.

From the bottom of my heart, thank you for taking the time to read this. Please let us know how you do with the process by contacting us at **www.hippycapitalist.com** or on Facebook at **https://rebrand.ly/hippycapitalistFB**.

ACKNOWLEDGEMENTS

To my loving wife Reka. Your support, advice, and contribution are nothing short of amazing. I am a better person because of you, your example, and support.

Thank you to my entire team for empowering us to live our dream of introducing one million people to a new way of thinking and impacting one million lives for the better. As a dyslecix author, I could not do it without you. You empower me to live our True North value of fearlessly giving first for the betterment of others. Thank you, thank you, thank you.

Perhaps most importantly, to all the brave, unemployed, underemployed, or miserably employed who are willing to take control of their lives by venturing on a treasure hunt to discover and create a life on their terms. Your example inspires me beyond words.

REFERENCES

1. *Burrows, S. (2017, September 22).* 85% of people hate their jobs, *Gallup* poll says [Blog post]. Retrieved from *https://returntonow.net/2017/09/22/85-people-hate-jobs-gallup-poll-says/.*

2. *Adams, S. (2013, October 10).* Unhappy employees outnumber happy ones by two to one worldwide. *Forbes.* Retrieved from *https://www.forbes.com/sites/susanadams/2013/10/10/unhappy-employees-outnumber-happy-ones-by-two-to-one-worldwide/#3b0d00a2362a.*

3. *Collins, J. & Porras, J. (1994).* Built to last: Successful habits of visionary companies (3rd ed.). New York, NY: Harper Business.

ABOUT THE AUTHOR

Kristopher Kluver is a seasoned entrepreneur, bestselling author, speaker, senior leadership advisor, mentor, and facilitator of business strategy consulting company. Kris started his first of 15 companies at age 19, just over 30 years ago. He has seen the innerworkings of hundreds of companies and has contributed countless hours of leadership team strategy facilitation. Kris is an Honorary Fellow at The University of York in the UK and has studied Entrepreneurial Strategy at Harvard Business School.

Embracing the lifestyle of the Hippy Capitalist, Kris has traveled to all seven continents, and met Reka while on a freighter in Patagonia. Later in life, he developed a new passion for endurance running and cycling events. Today, Kris and Reka enjoy helping others through their practices, writing, and videos. They dedicate three months of the year to adventure travel and personal growth.

You can learn more about Kris on YouTube and Facebook.

Kris & Reka